Medieval and Tudor Costume

Adam and Eve and their baby son, dressed in 12th-century styles. Adam wears a long tunic. Eve is in a long kirtle and veil head-dress; the baby is in swaddling clothes.

Frontispiece

Medieval and Tudor Costume

PHILLIS CUNNINGTON

Publishers

PLAYS, INC.

Boston

First published in 1968
by Faber and Faber Limited
3 Queen Square London WC1
All rights reserved
© Phillis Cunnington 1968
Published in Great Britain under the title
Your Book of Mediaeval and Tudor Costume
First American edition published by
Plays, Inc. 1968
Reprinted 1972

391
C917

Library of Congress Catalog Card Number
68–31593
ISBN 0 8238 0137 3

Printed in Great Britain by
Latimer Trend & Co Ltd Plymouth

ACKNOWLEDGEMENTS

The drawing of Lord Darnley and his brother on p. 42 is taken from *Children's Costume in England* by Phillis Cunnington, published by Messrs. A. & C. Black Ltd. A number of the other drawings are taken from *Handbook of English Mediaeval Costume* and *Handbook of English Costume in the 16th Century* by C. Willett Cunnington and Phillis Cunnington, published by Faber & Faber Ltd., and the frontispiece is taken from *The York Psalter in the Library of the Hunterian Museum, Glasgow* (Faber Library of Illuminated Manuscripts, T. S. R. Boase).

CONTENTS

INTRODUCTION

This book gives an account of the clothes worn by English men, women and children from the Norman Conquest to the end of Queen Elizabeth I's reign. For the sake of clearness, chapters or sections are arranged in centuries and for the sake of accuracy the pictures are copied from contemporary illustrations. Many of these drawings may look very unnatural, but it must be remembered that the Mediaeval artist, though highly skilled, had not studied anatomy and drew according to the style of his day. Many of the early pictures, too, are of a religious nature, being drawn by monks who, before the invention of printing, decorated 'illuminated manuscripts', that is illustrated books, written by hand. In the 13th and 14th centuries, the Psalter was a favourite in this country and usually consisted of a Calendar, followed by Psalms, Canticles and the Litany.

It will be noticed that early Mediaeval garments, both for men and women, were loose and flowing. Everything had to be made by hand, including of course the materials. Wool was largely used, though rich people wore linen or silk as well. Needles too were precious, and good steel needles had to be imported from specialist cities such as Nuremburg where it is on record that they were being made in 1370.

In spite, however, of all these difficulties in the making of clothes, definite fashions were followed throughout these centuries. But what is fashion and why do fashions change?

Introduction

Fashion may be defined as a taste shared by a large number of people for a short space of time. A taste persisting over a long period ceases to be a fashion and becomes a custom, such as the wearing of a skirt. Fashions change partly because no one likes monotony, but also because our clothes reflect ideas and ways of life which change with time.

Garments made for the convenience of the wearer or to indicate his trade seldom occurred during these centuries. The only protective wear was an apron. A woman would wear a gown with a train even when she was milking a cow.

A great change in fashion took place in the 16th century. A new world of wealth and learning was unfolding. A new aristocracy replaced many ancient families exterminated in the Wars of the Roses. The new styles gave men an artificial burliness and perhaps for the only time in our history men's fashions outshone and overpowered women's. No wonder Shakespeare said:

'The fashion wears out more apparel than the man.'
Much Ado About Nothing

MEN'S CLOTHES
11th, 12th and 13th Centuries

During the 11th and 12th centuries a man's suit consisted of a tunic and super-tunic (Fig. 1).

The tunic was a loose garment worn next to the shirt and generally put on over the head and worn with a waist belt or girdle. Some had side vents (slits), and a front vent was common in the 12th century. Knee length was usual but long tunics to the ankle were worn by older men and ceremonially.

The super-tunic worn over the tunic, probably for warmth as it was not an outdoor garment, was of similar design, though a little shorter than the tunic itself (Fig. 2).

Cloaks were worn out of doors and long mantles of fine material, often lined with fur, distinguished the nobility.

On their legs men wore loose pants called 'braies' (Fig. 3), of wool or linen, pulled in by a running string round the waist. Workmen might wear these long, like sloppy trousers, but by the 13th century they were shortened and became underpants only.

Stockings, called hose, were made of a strong woollen cloth (not knitted). They ended just below the knee and were kept up by tie garters or by leg bandages which were strips of linen bound spirally over the stockings. Criss-cross arrangement was popular with noblemen. On their feet men wore shoes or short boots of leather, tied with leather thongs (Fig. 4). Hose were sometimes soled with thin leather and could then be worn without shoes. All footwear had flat heels until James I's reign when heels began to be raised.

Headwear varied, the soft hood with the pointed cowl being the favourite (Fig. 5). It had a shoulder-length cape and was put on over the head with an opening for the face.

Large hats, often worn over the hood, and small round caps with short stalks were also common. A small cap with a pointed crown curving forwards was worn in the early 12th century. This cap was later referred to as the Phrygian bonnet (Fig. 6a and b).

Towards the end of the 12th century a close-fitting linen bonnet tied under the chin and called a coif was extremely popular and lasted for men till the end of the 15th century. They even wore it indoors (Fig. 7).

Gloves were worn by men of rank.

Men liked to have their hair curly (Fig. 1), often reaching down the neck, and beards, sometimes forked, were common with older men (Fig. 2).

During the 13th century country folk and peasants continued to wear the loose tunic and super-tunic, but these began to be replaced by rather better-fitting garments called cote and sur-cote respectively. The surcote was often sleeveless (Figs. 9, 10.)

Three new overgarments came into fashion which could be worn instead of the surcote. These were:

1. The tabard which consisted of a front and back panel with a wide neck opening and no sleeves. The open sides were sewn together at about waist level only. No belt was worn. This garment was the forerunner of the tabard worn by heralds.

2. The garde-corps was ample and long, having wide hanging sleeves with side slits for the arms to emerge for convenience sake. No belt was worn (Fig. 11).

3. The garnache. This, too, was loose and long with short shawl-like sleeves, and in the 14th century two tongue-shaped lapels were added. A belt was optional (Fig. 18).

There were no other obvious changes in the 13th century.

a   b

1. (a) Short embroidered tunic, cloak and criss-cross leg bandages. 11th century. (b) Man in short super-tunic, showing short tunic underneath, also cloak and leg bandages.

2. Long tunic, super-tunic and cloak. Hair style with forked beard.
11th century.

a   b

3. Braies (a) long, (b) short, and coif on head. (Detail) 12th century.

16

4. King in embroidered tunic, decorated hose, and shoes. Danes in countryfied clothes. *c.* 1125–50. 'St. Edmund is taken by the Danes' (Detail)

5. Rustic in short hooded cloak. The hood has a pointed cowl. 12th century.

a   b

6. (a) Short belted tunic and 'Phrygian' bonnet, also boots. 12th century
(b) Man wearing large hat. 12th century.

7. Coif with hood thrown back. 12th century.

8. Fishermen in short tunics, colours blue, red and buff. The bearded
man has white hair. 12th century.

9. Men wearing tunics, (cotes), and hats. One man on the tower is in a sleeveless surcote. (One man wields a flail.)

10. Sleeveless surcote, embroidered.

11. Man wearing a garde-corps with long hanging sleeves. His tunic has tight sleeves.

MEN'S CLOTHES
14th Century

The 13th century loose garments, still often called tunic and super-tunic, were worn by unfashionable folk and children to the end of the 14th century (Figs. 12, 13). Fashion, however, in Edward III's reign moved towards much better-fitting clothes and the gipon, soon to be called a doublet, replaced the cote.

The gipon at first was a close-fitting waisted garment reaching to just above the knees (Fig. 14). It had tight long sleeves and when worn with an overgarment had no belt. It was generally padded throughout and buttoned or laced down the front. Towards the end of the century it was called a doublet and was shortened to above mid-thigh and worn with a belt at hip level (Fig. 15).

A new overgarment was the cote-hardie, which lasted to the middle of the 15th century (Fig. 16). It was distinguished by having sleeves which ended at the bend of the elbow in front but continued into hanging flaps behind. These flaps gradually became longer and narrower and were merely ornamental. They were called tippets. A belt was sometimes worn.

Another new overgarment was the houppelande or gown (Fig. 17). It was very full and might be any length. When worn on ceremonial occasions it was long to the ground. The neck was high and the sleeves were long, loose and wide, though in the next century the pattern changed.

20

The garnache continued but now had two tongue-shaped lapels as already mentioned (Fig. 18). The tabard and garde-corps gradually went out of fashion.

Cloaks and shoulder capes were the usual outdoor wear to the end of the mediaeval period.

Men's stockings, or hose, were gradually lengthened and kept up by being tied to the doublet under its skirt. Shorter stockings were kept up by garters made of strips of wool or linen tied below the knee.

Short boots (Fig. 19) and shoes, later with instep straps, became fashionable (Fig. 20). Pattens began to be used towards the end of this century. They had wooden soles, raised under the heel and toe, and straps to fasten them on over the shoe. People wore them to keep their feet out of the mud.

Some new headwear now appeared. The popular hood continued but changed its shape. The pointed cowl was lengthened into a long streamer called a liripipe (Fig. 21) and from this another head-dress was made in the form of a turban with a fall-over flap made from the hood cape. This head-dress was called a chaperon (Fig. 22). Stalked caps were still common, also hats large or small. The small ones had a close turned-up brim. Towards the end of this century men began for the first time to wear feathers in their hats as a form of decoration. Gloves were now worn by all classes and those of field workers were curious, with a thumb and only two compartments for the fingers (Fig. 23).

12. Labourers in old-fashioned tunics. 1340.

13. The child David in a short tunic. Goliath in a loose surcote worn over his armour. The oldest church brasses in England show knights in this style of mail armour with a long surcote. Early 14th century.

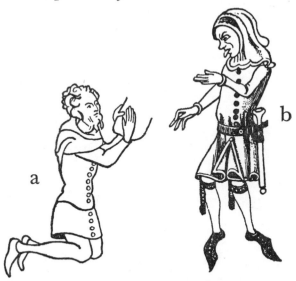

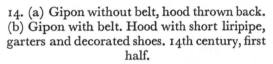

14. (a) Gipon without belt, hood thrown back. (b) Gipon with belt. Hood with short liripipe, garters and decorated shoes. 14th century, first half.

15. Gipon with belt worn round hips. Mantle fastened on right shoulder. (Stone effigy of Edward III's second son aged eight) 14th century, second half.

16. Musicians. Can you pick out the ones who are wearing cote-hardies?
1340.

17. Houppelandes, long and short. One man wearing piked soled hose, parti-coloured—that is each leg of a different colour. (Richard II's uncles.) *c.* 1395.

18. Garnache with shawl-like sleeves and tongue-shaped lapels. *c.* 1340.

19. Shepherd in old-fashioned tunic, short boots and hood with liripipe. 1380–99.

20. Shoes.

21. Men holding on to hammock wearing hoods with long liripipes; also belted gipons. 1340.

22. Two chaperons and a feather-trimmed hat. 14th century.

23. Peasants' gloves.

MEN'S CLOTHES
15th Century

The gipon, now called a doublet, lasted in different designs till towards the end of the 17th century (Fig. 24). In the 15th century it was close-fitting, waisted, very short-skirted and buttoned or laced in front. The belt was now worn at waist level. To begin with the doublet was collarless but soon a stand collar was added. It was generally covered by an over-garment, either a cote-hardie, a houppelande or later (*c.* 1450) a jacket or jerkin (Fig. 25), replacing the cote-hardie, which went out of fashion. The jacket was sometimes made with hanging sleeves or sleeves slashed on the outside to show the doublet sleeves underneath (Fig. 26). The houppelande or gown all through this century was sometimes made with bag-pipe sleeves (Fig. 27). These were closed round the wrist but had a huge hanging pouch often used as a pocket. This gown could be quite short, but was usually long to the ground and as such, with the hanging sleeves described later, was the fore-runner of university gown of today.

A great change took place in men's legwear, so that unlike the peasants and children, who continued in old-fashioned garments, a 15th-century gentleman was free from flapping skirts. His hose were joined above, combining stockings and pants to form tights (Fig. 24). These 'joined hose' were fastened to the doublet by leather ties known as 'points' and this is what the expression 'trussing the points' meant. There was

28

a front flap also tied by points and known as the 'codpiece'.

High boots, sometimes reaching above the knee, began to be worn and shoes with long pointed toes, known as piked shoes, were very fashionable from 1370–1410 and revived from about 1460–80. The pattens too followed this shape and were so much the vogue that they were worn indoors by the nobility (Fig. 28).

Hats, large and small, some made of beaver, were popular, and simple straw hats were worn by peasants. Caps were called bonnets and one shaped like a Turkish fez was known as a Turkey bonnet (Fig. 29b). The chaperon was going out of fashion and the hood was now mainly worn on horseback.

A very typical hairstyle for men was the 'bowl crop', as if a bowl had been placed on the head and the hair cut round it. Towards the end of the century, men let their hair grow long to the shoulders. The face was usually clean-shaven.

24. Short-skirted doublet laced across in front. Long hose with codpiece. *c.* 1479

29

25. Fisherman wearing a long-skirted jacket, with side vent and stand
collar. A chaperon on his head. 1460.

26. Jacket or jerkin with hanging sleeves.
1470–80.

30

27. Houppelandes—King Henry V with wide
fur-lined sleeves, Occleve, presenting his book,
wearing gown with bagpipe sleeves. Note his
hair in the bowl crop style. *c.* 1415.

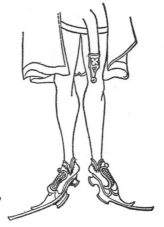

28. Piked shoes and pattens. 15th century,
second half.

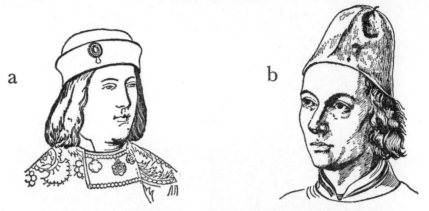

a   b

29. (a) Edward III in small round hat and long hair style, late 15th century. (b) Turkey bonnet. 1462.

30. Canterbury Pilgrims feasting at an inn. Note variety of headgear including the lady's steeple head-dress. 1483.

MEN'S CLOTHES
16th Century

The doublet was an indispensable garment throughout this period. The shape varied considerably. At first it had no collar and was made with or without a skirt, but by 1540 it had a standing collar and generally a short skirt (Fig. 31). It was usually fastened down the front by a close row of buttons, but some were laced, hooked or tied. A small waist with a tight belt was aimed at. From about 1570 it was fashionable to pad the lower front of the doublet so that it bulged over the belt. This was known as the 'peascod belly' (Fig. 32). ('Mr. Punch' in early numbers of the magazine was dressed to imitate this.) Sleeves were usually close-fitting, though sometimes very full. Stiffened welts called wings, often quite ornamental, were sewn round the armhole seam to hide the join from about 1540.

The jerkin or jacket, worn over the doublet, kept its shape throughout the various changes except for the sleeves which could be:

1. Close-fitting to the wrist.
2. Puffed-out shoulder sleeves.
3. Hanging sleeves which later became mere streamers.
4. Absent, represented by wings only (Figs. 33, 36).

A garment called a waistcoat was merely an under-doublet, usually sleeveless and worn for warmth.

The gown was very much worn (Fig. 34), and was often used as an outdoor garment until about 1545 when cloaks, having been rather neglected, came back into fashion again. The gown had full wide sleeves or hanging sleeves. (Compare academic gowns of today.) (Figs. 35, 36.)

Neckwear until 1545 was negligible, depending on a visible shirt collar, but after this date it burst into bloom, the most elaborate being the starched goffered frill known as the ruff. The ruff could be small, medium or large, spreading out from the top of the doublet collar in figure-of-eight convolutions. The large ruff was known as the cartwheel ruff (Fig. 37). These sometimes had to be supported on wire frames or on tabs turned out flat from the doublet collar and called 'picka-dils'. But when starch was introduced into England in the 1560's the ruffs were easier to manage. Some men preferred a turn-down collar to a ruff. This collar, which was turned down from a tall shirt collar, was called a falling band, band being the general term for a collar.

Legwear in this century went through many changes. The 'tights' (a descriptive term only) of the 15th century con-tinued, but the upper portion called 'upper stocks' or 'breech' began to be enormously distended and the whole garment was then called trunk hose (Fig. 38). The codpiece continued and was padded and prominent. From 1570 the thigh portions, called canions, were separated from the stockings which were pulled up over the canions (Fig. 39).

A major change took place, however, about the same time, when at last knee breeches came into existence. These gra-dually replaced trunk hose altogether. They varied in design, some being close-fitting with stockings pulled up over them and gartered above the knee, but most were very full and fastened below the knee. These were called Venetians and lasted till about 1620 (Figs. 40, 41).

34

Stockings, up till now, had been made of material cut on the cross, in order to get a good fit, but towards the end of Queen Elizabeth I's reign, knitting came to the rescue.

Footwear might be boots, long or short, and shoes. The toes were now so broad and square that in Henry VIII's reign an order was given limiting the width of the toe to six inches! (Fig. 42.) However, from 1540 on, toes were rounded. Pantofles were overshoes in the form of mules.

Hats and bonnets (i.e. caps) were generally worn indoors and always at meals until about 1680.

A very flat cap with a flat narrow brim was a popular style. By 1570 it was mainly worn by citizens and apprentices and was known as the City Flat Cap. Hat crowns were low at first but by the end of the century tall crowns were fashionable. The most famous was the copotain hat with a very tall crown and small brim (Fig 37).

'O fine villain! A silken doublet! A velvet hose! A scarlet cloak! and a copotain hat!'

Shakespeare—*The Taming of the Shrew*

Hair was usually long to the neck and beards were fashionable throughout this period.

Before leaving the 16th century a few words explaining the curious forms of decoration used on men's garments will be helpful.

Slashing meant slits made to show a white or coloured undergarment or lining. These slashes were sometimes arranged to form a pattern.

Pinking meant very very small slashes also making a pattern, and not what we mean by pinking today (Fig. 32).

Panes were long ribbon-like strips of material set close and parallel, so that a colour in between might be seen.

Embroidery too was much used on men's and women's garments. Towards the end of the century garments were sometimes embroidered not only with flowers, but also with designs of worms, flies, snakes and snails.

'Froggs and Flies for the Queen's Gloves' (1581) are on record.

Colours were usually very bright.

All through the period covered by this book, children, after babyhood, were dressed like their parents. Small boys wore skirts to their feet until reaching the age of seven or eight, when they were usually dressed like their fathers.

31. Robert Dudley, Earl of Leicester, his doublet decorated with pinking, has a short skirt, sleeves with wings and a high collar surmounted by a ruff. *c.* 1577.

32. Sir Philip Sidney—doublet decorated with slashing and pinking; also showing peascod belly. He has a ruff and hand ruffs. 1577.

wings

33. Sleeveless jerkin with wings only. The doublet sleeves are pinked. 1568.

34. Gown with full sleeves, faced and lined with fur.
Long hair style. 1507.

35. Prince, later King
Edward VI, in a short
gown with hanging sleeves
1541.

36. (a) Jerkin with wings. Trunk hose and codpiece. (b) Gown with hanging sleeves. A 'flat cap'. 1553.

a   b

37. Cartwheel ruff and copotain hat. 1586.

38. Lord Darnley in trunk hose, and his brother aged six in a long gown with winged sleeves and hand ruffs. Both wear ruffs. 1563.

39. Trunk hose with canions. The hair falling over his left shoulder was known as a 'love lock'. 1598.

B.C.P.

40. Sir Francis Drake—Venetians, i.e. breeches with stockings drawn over
and gartered above the knee. 1583.

41. Prince James, afterwards James I (aged eight)—Venetians fastened below the knee. 1574.

42. Henry VIII in broad-toed shoes. Gown with puffed sleeves, the doublet's sleeves protruding. Full-skirted jerkin, wide open over the chest to reveal the doublet. 1539.

45

WOMEN'S CLOTHES
11th, 12th and 13th Centuries

Like the men, women had a main body garment worn generally with an overgarment, but women's clothes were always long to the ground no matter what was their occupation, even when working out of doors or milking cows.

The tunic or kirtle, as it was called, was loose-fitting with long close-fitting sleeves (Fig. 43). In the 12th century ladies of rank began to have their kirtles made to fit the figure and the sleeves were sometimes expanded towards the wrists forming a sort of deep hanging cuff. Long sash-like girdles were usual. Under the kirtle only a chemise ('smock') was worn.

The super-tunic, worn over the kirtle except by women at work, was a rather voluminous garment put on over the head and worn without a girdle. The sleeves could be short to the elbow, but frequently of the hanging cuff style (Fig. 44).

Cloaks and mantles for outdoor wear were like those of men. Some cloaks had hoods attached (Fig. 45a and b).

Shoes also followed the men's styles.

Women's headwear all through the Middle Ages was distinctive and of importance to them. Only young girls might go without any head-covering, their locks hanging loose round their shoulders.

1. The veil, coverchief or kerchief, was a square or half-circle of linen, draped over the head, to fall in folds round the face and neck. It lasted to the end of the mediaeval period.

2. The wimple was not a head-covering. It was a strip of fine white linen (or silk for women of fashion) arranged so as to drape the front of the neck and chin, and then drawn up to frame the face, being pinned to the hair under the veil which was always worn with it (Figs. 46, 47).

3. At the end of the 12th century and lasting to the end of the 14th, a very popular head-dress known as the barbette and fillet came into fashion (Fig. 48). It consisted of a stiffened linen band encircling the head like a crown, with a similar band passing under the chin and encircling the face. This was often worn with a veil or, in the 13th century, over a hair-net.

Hair was mostly concealed by the headwear, but grand ladies in the 12th century sometimes wore two long plaits hanging down on either side.

High-ranking ladies made up their faces with paint.

Women in the 13th century continued wearing the kirtle, which was sometimes made with short slits called fitchets through which they could reach a purse slung from the waist underneath.

The super-tunic was now often called a surcote.

The headwear continued as before but a hair-net was very commonly worn with the barbette and fillet.

43. Super-tunic with wide sleeves worn over kirtle with narrow sleeves. Veil on head, mantle draped round shoulders and falling behind. 11th century.

44. Ladies in super-tunics with hanging cuffs. Kirtle sleeves just showing. 12th century.

45. (a) Fur-lined mantle over kirtle and veil on head. 13th century.
(b) Hooded cloak, embroidered super-tunic over tunic. 12th century.

46. Young girl in long kirtle and flowing hair. Lady in trained super-tunic
and wearing a wimple. Presumably she is negligée as the wimple was
never worn alone. Late 13th century.

47. Lady in veil and wimple. 12th century.

48. Barbette and fillet worn over net. Style of 13th and 14th centuries.

WOMEN'S CLOTHES
14th Century

The kirtle (Fig. 49), still sometimes called a tunic, continued unchanged until about 1330, after which it was shaped to the figure as far as the hips, ending in a long full skirt (Fig. 50b). The poet John Gower wrote:

> 'He seeth her shape forthwith all,
> Her body round, her middle small.'

Garments worn over the kirtle were:

1. The cote-hardie, figure-fitting but similar to that worn by men (Fig. 51).

2. The sleeved or sleeveless surcote which was loose, unshaped and long or sometimes ending just below the knees (Fig. 52).

3. The sideless surcoat, a very characteristic overgarment from about 1330. This was widely open at the sides from the shoulders to the hips (Fig. 53).

Out of doors, for travelling and riding, cloaks with hoods were worn. Ladies rode side-saddle, but even at this date country women sometimes rode astride.

Stockings were often brightly coloured, like those of Chaucer's Wife of Bath:

> 'Her hosen weren of fine skarlet redde.'

Probably owing to their long skirts, women do not appear to have worn piked shoes like the men.

Some new headwear appeared. One was an ornamental fillet looking rather like a coronet, and another was the chaplet, a padded ring which was worn over a hair-net. The veil was now often goffered (i.e. crimped) along one border and looked like a bonnet with the frilled edge framing the face (Fig. 54). Hoods and hats were worn for travelling.

A new hairstyle was to arrange two upright stiff plaits on either side of the cheeks (Fig. 55). These plaits were held in place by a fillet or coronet and sometimes worn with a veil as well. Hair was sometimes dyed saffron colour and make-up included painting and eyebrow plucking. A father who disapproved of this fashion wrote:

'Fair daughters, see that you pluck not away the hairs from your eyebrows, nor from your temples, nor from your foreheads, to make them appear higher than Nature ordained.'

(1371–2)

As regards 14th-century clothes, you will find that a visit to Westminster Abbey is very well worth while. There you have carvings of real people dressed in the style of their day. A good example is seen in the weepers (mourners) on the south side of the tomb of Edward III. Joan de la Tour wears a cotehardie, Mary Duchess of Brittany is in a sideless surcote and beside her is possibly the second son of Edward III, William of Hatfield, who is wearing a low-belted doublet. (Compare his effigy in York Minster—Fig. 15.)

49. Lady in loose kirtle and cloak. A barbette and fillet on her head. (Cloak mauve with green lining, kirtle pink.) Man and small boys in long tunics. *c.* 1320.

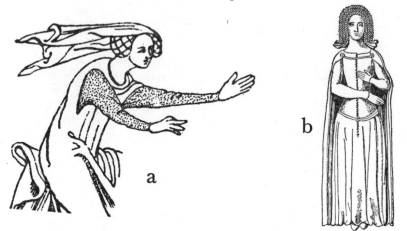

50. (a) Sideless surcote, flowing veil and hair net. 1340. (b) Well-fitting kirtle, laced down front. Long mantle, Goffered veil. (*For this see also Fig. 54.*) *c.* 1370.

53

51. Woman and man, either side, wearing cote-hardies; hers shows a fitchet, he has a hood thrown back, the liripipe hanging over his left shoulder. (In the centre St. Anne teaching the Virgin to read.) 14th century

52. Sleeved surcote. 14th century, first half.

53. Sideless surcote as worn in the 13th century. Tight kirtle sleeves buttoned. (From a monumental brass.)

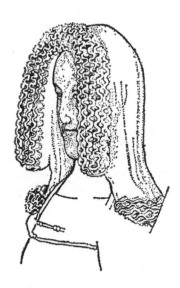

55. Hair style with upright plaits hugging the cheeks, supported by side pieces from the fillet. (From a monumental brass.) Style of 1340–1400.

54. Goffered veil. (From a monumental carving 1370.)

WOMEN'S CLOTHES
15th Century

The kirtle, worn next to the 'smock', close-fitting, with long tight sleeves often extending over the palms of the hands, continued as a woman's dress until about 1450 (Fig. 56). Soon after that date it was generally hidden by the gown, which now became a woman's ordinary dress.

The gown was long to the ground and gradually the waist-line was raised and marked by a belt which was often embroidered (Fig. 57). The sleeves were sometimes loose and widely open at the wrists, or rather baggy like the bagpipe sleeves of the past, or sometimes close-fitting.

The cote-hardie (Fig. 58) gradually went out of fashion and towards the end of this period the sideless surcote too was discarded except as State apparel. Hooded cloaks were still worn for travelling and so was the old-fashioned hood which, when worn by the gentry, was often lined with fur. The hood continued to be the outdoor headwear for the humble folk and peasants and it was also correct for funerals.

Indoor headwear was very important to fashionable women all through this century. Generally speaking it was low and wide during the first half of the 15th century and tall in the second.

A curious and popular head-dress was one known as the 'horned head-dress'. A writer of the time gave a description of a lady whose head-dress was 'horned like a cow'. This head-dress, combined with 'templets', soon to be described, was draped with a veil, spread over wires having the shape of a cow's horns (Fig. 59).

With various forms of headgear, the hair was often enclosed in jewelled cases on either side of the face, over or above the ears. These bosses were called templets as they hugged the temple (Fig. 60). There was usually a bit of drapery hanging behind as a sort of curtain.

Another head-dress was a circular padded roll which was later bent up forming a U-shape over the forehead (Figs. 61, 63).

During the tall period, the famous steeple-shaped head-dress called the 'hennin' came into fashion. It was introduced from France, but in England it scarcely ever ended in a sharp point. It was draped with a long gauze veil which hung down behind (Fig. 65).

A tall head-dress similar to the men's Turkey bonnet was also worn, with variations, by women (Fig. 62).

Another popular style, during the second half of this century, was the butterfly head-dress. It was made of a wire frame supporting a gauze veil which stood up above the head like two white wings. It was fixed to a small cap worn at the back of the head (Fig. 64).

Hair was almost completely hidden under these head-dresses.

Make-up with face painting and eyebrow plucking continued.

Shoes were similar to those worn by men, but never piked. Short boots called buskins were sometimes worn for travelling.

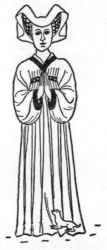

56. Kirtle, tight sleeves buttoned, and mantle. Note head-dress with templets. Brass. *c.* 1400. (*For these see also Figs. 59, 60.*)

57. Lady in high-waisted gown and veil draped over raised templets. *c.* 1430.

58. Young girl with flowing hair in cote-hardie with very long tippets; close-fitting kirtle sleeves. *c.* 1410.

59. Horned head-dress. (Monumental Brass.) 1416.

60. Templets. (Brass.) 1413.

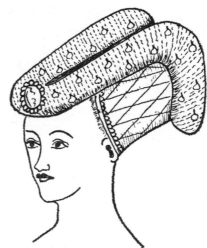

61. Padded roll head-dress curved upwards. 1450–60.

62. Turkey bonnet. 15th century, second half

63. Padded roll head-dress over veil. Style of late 14th and early 15th centuries.

64. Butterfly head-dress. (Brass.) 1482.

65. Caxton presenting one of his books to Margaret, Duchess of York, who wears a steeple head-dress. 1471.

WOMEN'S CLOTHES
16th Century

All through this century a woman's dress consisted of her gown and kirtle. The kirtle, meaning her dress, might be worn alone, but gown over kirtle generally made up the woman's costume. After 1545, when the bodice and skirt of both garments were made separately, the term kirtle came to mean the skirt only.

The gown continued to be loose and long until about 1545 when a great change took place, as will be seen from the illustrations. The bodice was stiffened with whalebone and the skirt usually made open in front with the $\wedge$-shaped gap through which the kirtle, or a decorative panel called a forepart, showed (Figs. 67, 68).

The hang of the skirt changed too, being distended by an underskirt lined with a series of hoops made of wood, wire or whalebone. This structure was called a 'farthingale'. There were two main styles, the Spanish which was dome-shaped, (Fig. 68) and the wheel or French which was tub-shaped (Fig. 69). A farthingale like this is worn by the recumbent figure of Sir John Pickering's wife (1596) in St. Paul's Chapel, Westminster Abbey. The Roll farthingale, popularly known as the Bum Roll, was merely a padded cushion, shaped like a life-belt, open in front, so that it could be tied on round the waist (Fig. 70). It was cheaper and less fashionable than the hooped farthingales and more worn by working women, who very often, however, did not trouble with any sort of farthingale (Fig. 76).

Like the men, women wore ruffs, small, large or medium according to the fashion. In addition a fan-shaped ruff which spread out round the back of the neck was worn with low-necked gowns (Fig. 69). The 'rebato' was a fan-shaped collar, wired to stand up round the back of the neck like the fan-shaped ruff. Ruffs were not always white. Some were coloured blue, some yellow. A foreign gentleman travelling in England in 1599 wrote:

'Now the women folk of England who have mostly blue grey eyes, and are fair and pretty . . . lay great store by ruffs and starch them blue so that their complexion shall appear the whiter.'

Another writer (P. Stubbs), who hated extravagant fashions, said:

'Then on toppes of these stately turrets (I meane their goodley heades . . .) stand their other capital ornaments, as French-hoode, hatte, cappe . . . and such like, whereof some be of velvet, some of taffatie, some (but few) of wooll.' 1585

He did at least tell us what sort of material was used for these head-dresses.

Hand ruffs were small frills at the wrist; turn-back cuffs were also worn.

Out of doors women still liked cloaks and towards the end of this period a 'safeguard' was an extra skirt worn as a protection from dirt and cold when riding; the 'lapmantle' was a rug serving the same purpose when travelling. Lapmantles are listed in Queen Elizabeth I's wardrobe in 1600.

Women's headwear during this century was very varied. Some of the old mediaeval head-dresses continued for a few years, but the new styles of indoor headwear are as follows:

1. The English Hood (1500–40) is distinguished by having a pointed arch wired up to frame the face and until *c.* 1525 showing the hair in the gap thus produced. It was generally edged by two long decorated flaps, while the drapery fell like a curtain over the shoulders behind (Fig. 71a). After 1525 these flaps were generally turned up and pinned at the top of the head, the curtain behind was made into two flat streamers, and the hair under the arch was concealed in two rolls (Fig. 71b).

2. The French Hood (1530–90) was a stiffened horseshoe-shaped bonnet worn far back on the head and tied under the chin (Fig. 71c). The curtain behind was generally a broad flap which was sometimes turned up to lie flat on the crown, with the straight edge projecting slightly over the forehead. When worn like this it was called a bongrace (Fig. 72). It was supposed to shade the face from the sun. It was sometimes a separate article which could be worn over a plain coif. Another protection for the face was an arched hood with a cape, and this was worn over the French hood (Fig. 73).

Out of doors hats, caps and bonnets were far less common at first than hoods, which were generally used for riding, travelling and country wear (Fig. 73).

The lettice cap was popular. Lettice was a fur resembling ermine and the cap was so shaped that it protected the ears from cold like a pixie cap (Fig. 75).

Low-crowned and tall-crowned hats were worn out of doors (Fig. 74).

The same foreigner who wrote about women's ruffs said:

'English burgher women usually wear high hats covered with velvet or silk for head gear.'   1599

The simple coif of linen was an undercap, but in this century it was worn by itself indoors, when it was often embroidered in coloured silks. The sides were made to curve forward over the ears, which gave it the nickname of 'cheeks and ears'.

Hair styles were rather hidden by headwear, but false hair, wigs and dyed hair were all in the fashion.

Black patches to show up the fairness of the skin just began to be used in 1595. Make-up with powder and paint was also practised. Ladies would put on masks to protect the complexion or even to act as a disguise.

With the introduction of knitting, women's stockings became much more interesting. What with the good fit and the bright colours used, gowns were often hitched up to show these elegant hose. Silk stockings were worn by the rich and fancy garters too were very popular, tied above or below the knee according to the length of the stocking. Elastic was unknown till the 19th century. The Lady Greensleeves had:

'. . . crimson stockings, all of silk [and] garters fringed with the gold.'   1584

Boots and shoes corresponded with those worn by men. Pumps were popular with women. Again the Lady Greensleeves had:

'. . . pumps, as white as was the milk.'

Amongst accessories, scented gloves, called 'sweet gloves', were popular with women, and, failing pockets, a number of

E   65

things might be suspended from the girdle by a ribbon or chain. These were a purse, a fan, a fur stole, a muff, a mirror, a rosary and a pomander. This last was a small jewelled box containing a perfume which was also supposed to protect from infection. One other item used for this purpose was the muffler (Fig. 76). It was a large square of material folded diagonally and swathed round the chin. It was also used as a disguise, for example to hide a beard!

> 'I spy a great beard under her muffler.'
> Shakespeare—*Merry Wives of Windsor*

Indoor lighting in those days was poor, so very bright colours were worn, especially among the upper classes.

All told, the fashions of the 16th century were broad, bold and burly. A man writing in 1605 about the English Nation said:

'When your posterity shall see our pictures, they shall think wee were foolishly proud of apparel.'

66. (a) Lady with swaddled twin babies. 1512. (b) Lady in gown with very wide sleeves, kirtle sleeves emerging. Both wear English hoods and rosaries. Style of 1500.

67. Forepart to skirt. Sleeves in a style very common at this date, wide
over-sleeves and large under-sleeves finished with chemise sleeve frill.
(Princess, afterwards Queen Elizabeth I, aged about twelve or thirteen.)
c. 1545.

68. Spanish farthingale. Also shows a forepart. 1560.

69. Wheel farthingale. Also shows long ornamental 'hanging sleeves' from the shoulder, a fan-shaped ruff and a wired up-standing 'band'. (Queen Elizabeth I.) 1592.

70. Lady being fitted with a bum-roll. Several lying about. *c.* 1599–1600.

71. (a) English hood early style. 1501. (b) English hood late style. 1527.
(c) French hood. *c.* 1540.

72. A bongrace. *c.* 1530.

73. Arched hood with shoulder cape. 1599.

74. Tall hat, feather-trimmed; gloves worn. 1573.

75. Lettice cap. 1527–8.

76. Working women without farthingales. The one on the right wears a
muffler and an apron. 1573.

INDEX

Index